ACCOUNTING

for

YOUR LIFE

Gina L. Thompson

Accounting for Your Life

www.accountingforyourlife.com

The following abbreviations are used to identify versions of the Bible used in this book:

KJV King James Version, also known as the Authorized Version (Public domain)

NLT New Living Translation, copyright © 1996, 2004, 2015 by Tyndale House Foundation. Used by permission of Tyndale House Publishers Inc., Carol Stream, Illinois 60188. All rights reserved. New Living, NLT, and the New Living Translation logo are registered trademarks of Tyndale House Publishers.

ISBN: 978-0-9995269-0-3
ISBN: 978-0-9995269-1-0

Contents

Introduction

"What are you passionate about?" After years of practicing accounting, I still struggled to find the appropriate response to this question. The question was often asked during career development discussions where I was expected to list with conviction the accounting positions that I aspired to attain. I always knew the answer to the question did not have anything to do with numbers, and I had an inkling that it had more to do with helping people. However, trying to define my career goals and match them with my passion had become what felt like an oxymoron. Accounting was my trade, but people were my passion.

While navigating this thing we call life, I discovered two things: 1) many of the concepts that I studied and applied in my accounting career also managed to apply to my life and 2) my every day is an accounting journal entry. As I began to identify my purpose and uncover the revelatory philosophy that our valuable lives need to be accounted for, I decided that this new perspective of life had to be shared with the world, so I wrote this book.

Whether or not you are a fan of numbers, this book is for you. As you read the pages, prepare to discover an unparalleled way of thinking and living. May your trajectory of success as the accountant of your life be so great that you leave an impactful legacy for generations to come.

This book is the marriage of my profession and my passion. Accounting is required for anything that has significant value, and my goal is to help you recognize that your life has an infinite value that requires disciplined accounting to foster truly successful living. May you too discover that your every day is an accounting journal entry.

Life Accounting Principles

This book is based on six fundamental *Life Accounting Principles*:

1) Every life as value.
2) Every day is an accounting journal entry.
3) Each journal entry impacts the accounts of life.
4) The accounts of life are impacted by decisions.

5) The transactions in life accounts determine the financial position of life.

6) Financial position is ultimately measured by fulfillment of purpose.

Practical Application

As you read this book, use the CERTIFIED LIFE ACCOUNTANT™ forms in the Appendix to assist you with practical application of these life accounting concepts.

CHAPTER ONE

Know Your Value

I cannot begin a book about accounting for one's life until I first establish the principle that every life has value. If you do not know or recognize that your life is a treasure and has infinite value, you may not see the importance of accounting for it.

Think about a small business such as a lemonade stand that earns about 50 dollars a year. It may not require a sophisticated level of accounting because of the perceived value, and we probably would not expect the lemonade stand owner to have an accountant on the payroll. On the contrary, a Fortune 500 corporation with billions of dollars will have an entire accounting department comprised of many qualified and certified accountants to ensure that the company's funds are properly accounted for. These accountants would define the company's stewardship, assist with growth projections and work to ensure financial stability.

From this general comparison, we can presume that the greater the perceived value or worth of a thing, the more attention and energy that is put into properly accounting for it.

What is your life worth to you? I would suggest that your life's value is immeasurable – priceless. Your life is so valuable that your Creator sent His only son to earth to die for you, because He saw that you and your future were worth dying for. On the contrary, tribulation, mistakes, comparison, and people may try to convince you that the value of your life is minuscule, but you should never believe or receive a misrepresentation of your life's value. Allow me to clarify some potential life misrepresentations: You are not a worthless failure who has nothing to offer in life. You are not insignificant or defined by your past. You are not limited by your looks or appearance. You are not only worth your family's economic status. You are not solely worth the value in your bank account. You are worth so much more. You were uniquely fashioned and formed by your Creator to be a solution and an answer to a need in the earth that only you can satisfy, to a void that only you can fill, and to a problem that only you can solve. Your style, your voice, your history, your passions, and your quirks all equate to your value, and in case you need to reread it – your value is infinite.

The progressive step after understanding your value, is accepting the responsibility to 1) love yourself 2) love the Creator of your value and 3) love your neighbor who may not yet recognize his or her value. In our current world, unfortunately, many of us have accepted the low value that man and culture have assigned us and allowed our discontent with our self-worth to dwindle our ability to love ourselves and to lead us on a path towards self-hate. In general, those on the path of self-hate get stuck in emotional ruts and struggle to find the freedom of love. These ruts can sometimes become places of confused comfort because they skew our ability to recognize that we deserve more. In addition, emotional ruts limit one's capacity to receive love or give love to others. They also cause hurt people to hurt others with a false hope that putting others down increases intrinsic value. Ruts could be the very reason that our world seems to be experiencing a love disparity despite the fact that we were created by Love.

So, how do you value your life? Have you managed to escape the value-obscuring emotional ruts formed by negative rhetoric, abandonment, and disappointment? Embracing your eternal identity and understanding that you have something unique to offer this world that no one else has should be the basis of your self-value. Your Creator did not make a mistake when He hand crafted and formed you. He made you special. You are so unique and essential that Love cares about your inner most being, gives you purpose and provision, and calls you royalty. This is why I can conclude that you are in fact a treasure and your life has infinite value.

If you haven't already, you can accept the intrinsic value that your Creator has given you by saying this prayer:

Father, I declare that the generational curse of self-hate is broken. I repent for not understanding and accepting the value that you have given me. Today, I see that I am worth your love. I accept that I am priceless, and I desire to be a good steward of this valuable life that you have given me. I declare that I am rich in you, rich in joy and rich in love, and I have plenty left over to share with others. Thank you for your grace. Amen.

Now that we have established your value, we can delve into why you purchased this book. Let's talk accounting. From beginning to end, my goal in writing this book is to give you a clear understanding of accounting principles that you can use to manage your personal or business finances while also giving you the practical application of how the same accounting principles can also guide how you manage your life.

CHAPTER TWO

Accounting 101

Introduction

What is accounting? I've heard variations of the word "account" in different contexts throughout my life. The first form that comes to mind is: "You will be held *accountable* for your behavior." This was in my teenage years, but it resonated with me throughout my time in college and thereafter. It drove me to host a spirit of excellence in my work ethic because if I was going to be held accountable, I wanted good results, zero punishment, and positive consequences. The second form of the word "account" that comes to mind is when I opened my first *bank account*. It was something that I had ownership of and could either add to or deplete. Later in high school, I was exposed to the last form of the word "account" that I will describe. I learned that in the financial world, there are a plethora of *accounts* that are used to classify the financial factors of a business. Throughout this book, we will explore these accounts both literally and figuratively.

Now that we have explored some variations of the word, what does accounting mean? According to Dictionary.com, accounting is the "art of analyzing the financial position and operating results of a business [house] from a study of its impacting transactions." That's a long definition, but here are the main points that I find are necessary to define accounting: 1) It's an art. 2) It relates to position. 3) It has results.

1) It's an art.

I assume you are thinking that there is nothing artistic about accounting, but I believe that accountants are in fact artists in their own rights. Just as artists create, accountants create accounts and think analytically when evaluating the effects of accounting transactions.

2) It relates to position.

Accounting yields position. When a company makes good accounting decisions, they increase their chances of having a solid accounting position, and conversely, when a company makes bad accounting decisions, they may find themselves in a poor financial position.

3) It has results.

Accounting is used to summarize the financial results of a business's operations. Most decisions and transactions yield a financial result, and as accountants, we should be able to forecast and understand these results.

Accounting is something that every person can benefit from understanding because anywhere there is money or value, accounting is necessary. Throughout this book, I strive to make the complex concepts of accounting simple and relatable, and I hope your understanding of the technical aspects of accounting will set a foundation for the figurative philosophy of accounting. My hope is that you not only gain a working knowledge and understanding of accounting from a financial perspective, but that you also feel equipped and certified to account for your own life. Just as transactions affect the financial position of a corporation, our decisions and actions impact the quality of our lives.

Debits and Credits

In the financial accounting world, there are two terms that are universal: debit and credit. Whether you are on a beach in Hawaii, riding with the bulls in Spain or skiing on Mt. Everest, these two terms have the same meaning. From a technical perspective, one could use colossal literation to elucidate the conceptual philosophy of debits vs. credits, but I will spare you a headache and explain it to you simply. You see what I did there? So here it is: Debit means left; credit means right. This will all make perfect sense soon, but the key is as long as you remember debit means left, and credit means right, you are pretty much guaranteed to understand this concept. So, as I was describing the different uses of the word account at the beginning of this chapter, I mentioned that the financial world has a plethora of accounts that are used to classify financial factors of a business. Some examples of these accounts are cash, receivables, liabilities, expenses, and revenues. Each account either has a "debit" balance or a "credit" balance. If an account has a debit balance that means that items are *added* to the account on the *left* side. Hence, debit=left. The opposite of this is also true. Items are *subtracted* from accounts with a debit balance on the *right* side. This also means that for accounts with a credit balance, items are *added* on the *right* side and *subtracted* on the *left* side. As long as you remember debit=left and credit=right, you are ready to take the next step on this accounting journey. I will delve into the types of accounts that have debit balances and credit balances a little later, but for now, knowing your left from right is the fundamental understanding of debits and credits.

A=L+E

I know some people become easily intimidated by the word "accounting" because they think it involves a lot of math, numbers, and complex equations that are hard to remember. Well, let me clarify the rumors and share that there is hope for everyone to master the art of accounting both in practice and in life because there is only one key equation that governs accounting. The equation is Assets = Liabilities + Equity, also known as A=L+E. A=L+E is as easy as A=B+C: "A"ll mine= "B"etter pay + "C"apital Stewardship. From a financial perspective, assets include accounts such as cash, accounts receivable, prepaid, and fixed assets. These are accounts that "add value" and that are owned by an individual or company; hence, "All mine." Liabilities are accounts such as accounts payable, accruals and deferred income, which represent amounts owed by an individual or company. These are things they "Better Pay." Lastly, equity is the ownership in the company. It includes the initial investment and is secondarily impacted by the revenues and expenses incurred. In terms of the equation, equity is what is left after subtracting the liabilities (what is owed) from the assets (what is owned). Effective "Capital Stewardship" is required to ensure you have positive (and not negative) equity.

Debits and credits along with the accounting equation are the two foundational concepts that are needed for understanding accounting. Since you are well versed in both concepts, let's combine them. Assets always have a debit balance. Liabilities always have a credit balance. In regards to equity, revenues have credit balances, and expenses have debit balances. The next concept in this theory of accounting is that debits should always equal credits. You may have heard Sir Isaac Newton's Third Law of Motion: "that for every, action there is an equal and opposite reaction." Well, the same statement is true for accounting. Every transaction causes both a debit and a credit to an account. Let's test this concept. If you pay cash for a new car, you inherently are creating a transaction between two assets: decreasing cash (an asset) and increasing another asset (the car); thus, creating a credit to a cash account and a debit to the car asset account. That's how one transaction creates both a debit and credit. Here's one more example. Let's say that instead of paying cash for the car, you took out a loan. The debit would still be to the car asset that you gained, but the credit would now go to an accounts payable or liability account, because you now owe the lender for the cost. Again, the transaction creates both a debit and credit.

I find it necessary to dig a little deeper into these aspects of the accounting equation, because they are the foundation needed for you to master the ability to account for your life effectively. So here is a little more insight into these three key concepts: Assets, Liabilities, and Equity.

Assets

As explained earlier, assets are items that add value to the company or individual. I like to think of assets as things that are "All mine." Whether it be your cash on hand, personal investments, items owed to you (known as accounts receivable), your home, or land, assets add value to a financial status or position. Assets also give you negotiating power. As much as we may hate to admit that money makes the world go around, we cannot ignore the fact that the person with the dollar typically has the front row seat and in most cases, the driver's seat of influence. Although this book is not your guide to a monetarily rich life, may you find that your value puts you in the driver's seat of your life. From life's perspective, your assets are represented by your uniqueness, your loving family, your supportive friends, and your values. These are all factors that make you who you are. Furthermore, who you are determines the fruit you produce, which can add even more value to your life. To be clear, I do not mean fruit in the natural sense (although I love a sweet and juicy strawberry). Spiritually, your fruitfulness is measured by the amount of love, joy, peace, patience, kindness, goodness, faithfulness, gentleness, and self-control you display (Galatians 5:22-23 NLT). We are recognized and identified by the fruit that we produce in our lives (Matthew 7:16a NLT). We have an entire chapter on Assets later on, but for now think about a few things: How much value are you currently exhibiting? What kind of fruit are you producing? As the accountant of your life, it is imperative that you assess your current financial position. How many assets do you have? How much are they worth? Do you have growth opportunities?

Liabilities

Liabilities are items that you owe to someone else. From a financial perspective, this could be cash that you need to pay someone for a good or service that you received in the past. It could also be a service or good that you need to deliver because you have already received money for it in advance. Liabilities are financial obligations, and although they are widely accepted in the corporate world, they must be managed closely, because a business that has little financial leverage may raise questions concerning their ability to continue in business. In our lives, liabilities are things that we "Better pay" if not today, it needs to be handled tomorrow. In life's view, these obligations and liabilities could be represented by owing an apology, forgiveness, obedience, or love. Because of grace, we can still have a balanced equation if we have liabilities, but the fewer liabilities we have, the greater our total ownership (equity) will be. Again, we have an entire chapter on liabilities ahead, but for now ask yourself: What are my liabilities? Do I owe something to someone? Do I owe something to myself?

Equity

Equity represents stability. Although start-up companies are expected to experience negative equity in the beginning due to the focus being on borrowing or paying what is needed to launch or giving bigger discounts to get product tries, mature companies must maintain positive equity in order to provide dividends to the shareholders who have invested in them. Equity is our capital stewardship. In life's view, it is the reconciliation of our life with our Creator's purpose for us. Equity is our measurement of self-actualization, and it is vastly affected by life's revenues and expenses. Revenues are the victories in life and expenses are failures. As personal accountants of our lives, we must manage our accounting position to ensure that we are winning as individuals on a daily basis. For example, when our patience is tested by the person who cuts us off on the highway, do we win by remaining calm, being thankful that they did not hit and injure us, and hoping for their safety? I know it can be difficult, but the key to managing revenues and expenses is being present. We have to recognize tests, attacks, and negative experiences and not allow them to have power over our responses, as our responses may impact the equity of our lives. What would you say is the current value of your personal equity?

Now that we have a clearer understanding of the accounting concepts and how they translate to our lives, let's delve into specific situations in our lives and how they can affect the accounting equation of our lives. We will explore whether certain events will debit or credit our accounts and how the debits and credits affect our ownership and equity. From a financial perspective, it is nice to have assets on hand that can readily be available to cover liabilities. It is also important to have more revenues than expenses, so that equity remains positive. As individuals desiring to effectively account for our lives, our ultimate goal should be to have our assets equal our equity. Liabilities are the things that we want to work on minimizing from day to day. We also want to gain lots of revenues and have very few expenses, so that our equity can be positive. Now, I must be completely honest, because we do not live in a vacuum, this balance is not as easy to achieve, but this is why it is important that we understand the need to account for our lives. If we make a conscious effort to increase our assets and revenues and decrease our liabilities and expenses, then we will achieve the capital stewardship that our Creator intended for us when he created us. Remember our Creator had three things in mind when he created us: To be fruitful. To multiply. To have dominion. (Genesis 1:28 KJV) Properly accounting for our lives will help us to produce spiritual fruits, to grow and live in abundance.

CHAPTER THREE

Mindset Shift

A s you can tell already, accounting is an entirely different way of thinking. Debits, credits, and accounting lingo demand an intentional focus. This is why you find that some of the most successful accountants are analytical, critical thinkers. In the same parallel, as life accountants, it would be challenging to pick up a pencil and begin accounting for our lives without first having a mindset shift. What I mean by mindset shift is that we have to ensure we establish the necessary thought process that will support our success in accounting for our lives. Our mind and thoughts have so much influence over the rest of our lives. Our emotions, feelings, actions all stem from our thoughts, so if our goal is to affect our actions by accounting for our lives, we must ensure that our thoughts are in alignment. Otherwise, our efforts may not be as successful. For as a man thinks in his heart, so is he (Proverbs 23:7a KJV).

Knowing that each life to be accounted for has three key facets: mind, body, and spirit, let's give this book permission to impact how we think about these aspects. We should consider what we are thinking, how we treat our bodies and the spiritual impact of our decisions. Our minds alone can take us from a place of peace to a place of fear. Thoughts can create confusion or define purpose. Because we were formed and fashioned into unique vessels often referred to as bodies, the thoughts in our mind can give us the confidence to control our bodies and the capacity to live fulfilled lives. Because our spirit is what sustains us, makes us whole, and helps us to remain centered in life, we should allow our spirit to guide our thoughts, as well. We have an accountability to manage our lives in a manner that keeps our minds stable, our bodies healthy, and our spirits strong. A mindset that is committed to getting the most out of life – mind, body, spirit – is a mindset that will propel you forward in this process of accounting for your life.

So, if your mindset needs a little tweak or adjustment, here is an opportunity to channel all thoughts of focus, success, and completion. Failing is never an option, and there is no need to be intimidated or fearful, because you were born with the power and ability to adequately account for your life. Think progress and fulfillment. Although total fulfillment of destiny may take a lifetime, progress can be achieved every day that we wake up and choose to be the accountants of our lives. Accounting for every decision, response, action, and reaction is not intended to criticize ourselves or highlight where we struggle. Accounting helps us to know where we are and make intentional decisions to transfer us to where we would like to be. As you read these accounting concepts, an appropriate mindset to have is: "I will become the best accountant of my valuable life."

Chapter Four

I Like My Assets

So, let's talk about assets. As mentioned earlier, assets are the things that a business owns. This includes cash, which gives the capacity to purchase additional assets or invest into the business. Another common asset is what is described a prepaid asset, and this is the value that represents goods or services that you have paid for, but not yet received. Inventory is another common asset in a business which is the product on hand that the business plans to sell for revenue and income at a future time. The last asset that I will describe, as these are the most common, is accounts receivable. Accounts receivable includes the value of services or goods provided to a customer that they have not yet paid for. In short, accounts receivables are monies owed to the business.

As you can see from the business perspective an asset is something of value that is owned, in your possession or owed to you. In our individual lives, we can identify our assets by noting the valuable things that we have. From a financial perspective, our financial assets can include the cash in our bank accounts, property that we own such as a house, a car, or a boat. Another personal financial asset can be a personal investment such as stock in a company.

Because I can't have a book about accounting and not talk about money, I will quickly give you my perspective on how to manage the asset we refer to as cash in our personal lives. What do you do with your cash? Do you spend it, save it, give it, or invest it? I would suggest that the personal accountant that answers yes to all four of these options in proportional moderation is wisely managing their cash account.

Spend it.

Spending money puts money back into the economy so that your country can thrive and flourish. This benefit of spending is not a license to spend everything and does not mean shop until you have no money left; however, responsible citizens do spend money, whether it is to pay taxes, pay bills timely, or buy necessities. Spending money is inevitable and necessary; the important thing to remember about spending money is to incorporate discipline while spending. One thing that can help develop a disciplined mindset in regards to spending is creating a budget. Essentially, a budget is a plan for your money, and it is only effective if two factors are in place: 1) The budget must be reasonable for your income, and 2) You must adhere to your budget. If you budget for a monthly vacation, a weekly car wash, and dining out daily, but do not have enough money to cover bills and other necessities, then although you have it in a budget, it is not conducive for your current financial position. An unbalanced budget will do more harm than good. As the accountant of your life, wise and disciplined decisions must be made regarding what to include in your budget. Also, even the most disciplined budget is ineffective if it is not executed. Today, advanced technology has made it convenient for us to develop and track progress against budgets electronically, and as accountants, we should use such tools to ensure that we do not allow our actual spending to exceed our budget.

Save it.

Although spending is necessary, it is not a necessity to spend all of your money at once. What happens if your only transportation to work fails? Or an unexpected operation cannot be put on hold? Will you have the cash to cover it? What if you suddenly become unemployed? These "what if" questions are the primary reason to establish a hearty savings account. Because everyone is at different places in their lives, I suggest starting with something comfortable for you. You should strive to save regularly, but do not save so much that you do not have enough money to spend on the aforementioned necessities of life. Saving is the safe-haven that keeps you from having to stress when the unexpected happens. In addition, saving for known future costs such as retirement, vacation, or education for children relieves the burden of having to come up with money on the spot. Time is your friend when it comes to saving, because the sooner you begin to save, the more you can accumulate over time. As your own personal accountant, if you have not already, please open a savings account today and begin to save for your future.

Give it.

I probably should have started with this cash activity, because it will likely determine how much you will have left to spend or save. How much you give is a direct indicator of how much you will receive. There is no deep, philosophical way of explaining this other than – like the law of gravity, it is a law of giving established by our Creator, that if you give, it will be given to you good measure pressed down shaken together and running over" (Luke 6:38a KJV). While accounting for my life, I have learned that giving with wisdom and out of obedience has even greater returns than simply giving to receive, but I encourage you to explore giving for yourself and see how it works for you.

Invest it.

If you moderately and proportionately exercise the first three cash activities of spending, saving, and giving, you will likely find that you still have money left over for investing. I know some people are apprehensive and may have a fleeting trust in "Wall Street," but wise investments have the potential to cause your money to grow exponentially. Consider seeking out investment experts for guidance on how to and where to invest. It is also worth noting that an appreciating asset such as a house can also be considered a good investment.

This concludes my thoughts on the most common asset, cash, and because I believe you bought this book to read more about accounting for your personal life than managing your wallet, I will continue this chapter of exploring assets with discussing the personal assets of our lives. Some forms of personal assets that can add value to our lives are relationships, time, confidence, education, and spirituality.

Relationships.

When I began to reflect on the assets that add value to my own life, the first thoughts that came to mind were family, friends, mentors, and accountability partners. Consequently, they all fall under the relationship umbrella, but not all relationships are necessarily assets. So, to be clear, *healthy* relationships are assets that add value to our lives, and we should seek out and maintain such relationships as life accountants.

Relationships are great. They are institutions that we can give and receive from. Whether it be kind words, support, or a simple hug, relationships may come and go, but the value of them is pertinent in our equation of life.

Business.

I'll start with business relationships. These are the relationships we have with our bosses, coworkers, or within our business network. These relationships may not necessarily result in heart-wrenching conversations or emotional syntax, but how you relate via e-mails, calls, and meetings may strongly affect your next business move.

In part, work relationships can determine whether you stay at a certain job. If the relationship is unhealthy, you may find yourself searching for a new job sooner than ideal, or if the relationship is supportive, you may stay for comfort and validation. How do we manage business relationships in a manner that gives balance to our relationship account? Communication. I have found that it is important to communicate your goals and ideas in business relationships. Now, I am not suggesting that you go to work on the first day and tell your boss you plan to leave within a year to pursue better opportunities. However, communicating the skills that you would like to obtain while in the position will forever be an unknown if you don't state it to the right people. It is also helpful to communicate your accomplishments, goals, and values, because people do not know what you do not tell them. If you do not communicate in a business relationship, people will develop their own opinions about you, your intentions and your opportunities based on their perception of you. In today's world perception trumps reality. If we are not intentionally communicating, we permit others to assume their misperceptions are true. To be honest, even after you communicate, some people will still have a closed mind to your truth, but at least you have communicated and shared your truth. The next step after communicating is to live your truth and be the best you on your job that you can be, because even if the working relationship is not the best, your work output can never be denied.

I am not sure why, but I always found it so easy to gossip at work. It may have been because there was so much to talk about. Whether it was discontent with treatment, the desire to have more flexibility, or the need for a culture of inclusiveness, there was always something to "discuss." Gossiping, discussing, or complaining (whatever you prefer to call it) to your co-workers about what you do not like will NOT change anything; yet again, communication is your friend because bringing new ideas and options to a business meeting with the right attitude could get you recognition for innovative and strategic thought. You may not see immediate results, but speaking up may make things easier for those who come after you. Like all relationships, business relationships require management from you as the accountant of your life. Managing how, when, and what to communicate can lead you to success.

Friendship.

Friendship is another form of a relationship that can impact your life equation positively. Are you a good friend? Do you have good friends? There are two laws of friendship from our Creator that I'd like to highlight. 1) As iron sharpens iron so does one man sharpen another (Proverbs 27:17 KJV) and 2) he who has friends must show himself friendly (Proverbs 18:24 KJV).

In essence, healthy friendships are two-fold. You give love and receive love. You give support and receive support. Trust and respect are mutual, and the truth is glorified in healthy friendships. A true friend will make you a better you. You can count on good friends to be there when everyone else is self-occupied, and you can share your inner most secrets with good friends without fear of judgment. A good and true friend that is an asset that will cheer for you when you excel and help you to get back on track if you fall short. Do you have friends in your life that meet this description? As a child, having a lot of friends was my desire, but in my adult life, I have found that a few good and true friends is far more valuable. Friendship is a quality over quantity thing for me now. I would rather have a few friends that I can count on than a lot of "friends" who are never there. As life accountants, we should manage our friendship asset account. We can manage it by debiting the account as we find good friends. I have found that the key to finding good friends is to be a good friend to others. Being a good friend can attract good quality friends. In addition, you will be able to assess friendships better if you know what to look for in them. During your friendship account management, you may also find that some of your "friends" are not really your friends. My suggestion is: Love them, and let them go because a friend that is not an asset is a friend that is a liability. In our quest to account for our lives in a manner that results in increased equity, we must make some difficult decisions such as laying aside every weight (or liability) that could so easily beset us (Hebrews 12:1 KJV). If you have identified toxic and draining friends, it is okay to let them go. As we manage our lives, we cannot allow everyone to have access to our asset accounts. Some people will deplete us, if we don't let them go. I know it is much easier said than done, but think about your life, your value, and your purpose. You cannot afford to have leeches as friends. Be kind to everyone, but be selective with your circle of friends; your life asset account depends on it.

Mentors and Accountability Partners.

Mentors and accountability partners are the final relationship asset that I will discuss. A mentor is generally a person who has experienced more in life than you have yet to experience, and they are willing to share the wisdom they have obtained with you. Mentors can listen, advise and connect you with other great resources. It can be helpful to have multiple mentors for different aspects of your life such as academic, career, and spirituality. As the accountant of your own life, it is your responsibility to seek out mentorship by identifying and asking a reputable person to become your mentor. It is also your responsibility to define what you expect from the mentorship. Whether it is meeting quarterly in person or monthly check-ins over the phone, it is best to set clear expectations of what you need from the mentorship.

Accountability partners are generally in your peer group and in similar stages in life. These are individuals that you share your goals and progress with and ask them to hold you accountable along the journey of trying to reach your goals. You can also have multiple accountability partners for different goals or areas of your life. The key for managing the accountability partner asset account is clear communication. You have to communicate what you want to be held accountable for, and your accountability partner must communicate to you when you are not progressing. In my life, accountability partners provide the nudge that moves me from a state of indolence to a mindset of determined progress. Both mentors and accountability partners add value to your life and have the potential to make you a better you, if you utilize the resources appropriately.

Time.

Time is another asset that gives us the capacity to enjoy and make the most of our lives, but as accountants, we should be mindful of the balance in this time asset account. Time is not infinite, so we have to be very selective on how we spend and invest our time to ensure that we are getting the most out of life.

In heaven, life is eternal, but here on earth our time as limitations. Since we know that our time on earth is limited, it is very important to account for our use of time. A renowned psalmist once wrote, "Teach us to number our days" (Psalm 90:12 KJV). I believe this was a request to learn how to appropriately manage and account for time. Managing the time account is about understanding that because time is finite, we should use wisdom when determining how to spend our time. For the most successful life accountants, most of their time is spent on things that last for eternity. To reach this level of success, we need to make some changes in the way that we account for our time here on earth. The biggest change is setting a goal to spend our time on earth doing things that will outlast our time here. We should be intentional about ensuring that our actions on earth have value in the infinite realm of heaven where time is endless. Of course, we have obligations on earth that require time and only impact our limited time on earth, but our time can be maximized if we focus on the "how" when doing those things. For example, I have to go to work for eight hours of the day, and that is time that cannot be replaced or retrieved. I can, however, make a conscious effort to focus on how I do my job and to interact with others on my job in a way that can make an endless impact. Whether it is sharing unconditional love, helping others, or displaying an infectious joy, these are all things that tap into the infinite realm and leave lasting impressions even after an assignment is complete. Almost anyone can complete a job, but the lasting impressions we leave are a result of how we complete the work and how we make others feel along the way. There is a quote by Carl W. Buehner that mentions how people will forget what you said, but they will never forget how you make them feel. I believe this quote embodies the importance of accounting for time in a way that balances finite activities with infinite impact.

What are we doing with our limited time on earth that will be impactful for eternity? We may not have all the answers today, but if we account for our lives in every area as it has been outlined in this book, we will likely begin to make time investments that will maximize our eternal impact. Time is the one asset that we do not want to waste because we cannot control the debits to the account. All our decisions regarding time relate to its use, so as life accountants, let's be intentional about using our time wisely.

Confidence.

Confidence is an asset that you can have that will impact how you live and interact with others, and it will be evident in how you carry yourself. Studies show that women may struggle with this more than men struggle; however, a confidence struggle is not a rarity nor is it a hopeless end. You can build confidence by preparation, self-affirmation, and confirmation. Alan Lakein once said that failing to plan is planning to fail. If you want to experience victory in your life, it is imperative that you prepare. If you have prepared, you are much more likely to execute with confidence and ease. This is something that I have practiced in my career. Whenever I had a presentation opportunity, I would prepare my presentation, pre-plan my remarks and practice answering questions that I anticipated would be asked. I may have spent day and night practicing in front of family, friends, and co-workers, but when the moment to present came, I was ready. I would get feedback from the audience saying that I was great and did not seem nervous at all. They perceived confidence, but I would venture to say that they actually saw evidence of my preparation. If I had not practiced and prepared, that confidence would have quickly withered away.

Self-affirmation is another confidence building technique that I use frequently. Whether it is reciting "I AM" statements, looking in the mirror saying "I CAN," or reading Biblical promises aloud, hearing yourself speak positively about your today and your future brings about assurance and confidence. If you do not say great things about yourself, how can you ever expect others to say great things about you? As the accountant of your life, you should ensure that you are doing all that you can to debit your asset accounts, and because your words carry power, telling yourself that you are great can help build your confidence and increase your asset value.

Lastly, confirmation is a technique to build confidence within yourself. Confirmation is when you create small wins. These are opportunities to accomplish baby step victories. Even though these are not your biggest accomplishments, the fact that you are successful at them can confirm your positive thoughts about yourself and continue to build your confidence. Having patience with yourself and your progress by starting small is not synonymous with being lazy; it is simply a technique to prove to yourself that you can finish, complete, and perhaps do more. For example, if your goal is to lose 10 pounds in 3 months, set the goal to lose 1 pound in 1 week. If you execute your plan and are successful with the 1 pound, you now have confirmation that your plan is working *and* confidence that you can meet and possibly even exceed your expectations in future weeks. Accomplishments, whether great or small, build confidence and impact the attitude you bring to the next assignment. This is why confidence is such an important asset.

As managers of this asset account, your goal should be to strive daily to increase this account. A confident person who executes is an individual who attracts, whereas a person who lacks confidence is more likely to project negativity on others. Confidence does not make you untouchable; it makes you attractive. Confident people attract other positively confident people, because confident people are easier to collaborate with, as they are not in a constant unannounced battle to prove themselves to be better than the next person. Confident people are comfortable in their own skin and know that they have something to offer the world that no one else has; however, they also recognize that everyone has something special and unique to offer. Confident people know how to run their race and not be distracted by the accomplishments of others. Confident people are finishers. As the accountant for your life, it is imperative that *you* continue to increase your confidence account. Confidence is internally driven. If confidence is built by external forces such as people telling you that you are great, it will quickly fade when people stop complimenting you. For confidence to be sustainable, it must come from within you. You should be the only authorized signer on your confidence account. This means that only you can add to or take away from the account. Truly confident people are not impacted by the opinions of others because they walk in their own truth and manage their confidence account.

Education.

Education is another personal asset. When you are educated, it adds tools to your toolbox that equip you for even greater wins. The more you learn, the more information you have to apply to your life. This is not to say that uneducated individuals are lacking and cannot win in life; however, I would encourage us all to seek out books or even classes that can provide information and insights to help us continue to be successful. When we decide to educate ourselves, we can avoid some mistakes and make better-informed decisions. As your life's accountant, you can manage or increase the value of your education account by setting reasonable goals to read a certain number of books or complete a certain degree or certification. Another valuable trait of education is that it is an asset account that external factors cannot credit or deplete. What you have invested time and resources in learning is yours forever. The key to managing this account is to be intentional about adequately and appropriately applying the knowledge that you have obtained. Knowledge can produce wise decisions, give you influence, and position you to help others, but when knowledge is not utilized, it can become dormant. As you manage this account, always seek out ways to apply the new knowledge that you obtain.

Spirituality.

Finally, spirituality is my favorite asset because it can in many ways impact and increase all other asset accounts. When we are centered and connected to our spiritual being, we are positioned to receive the most out of our lives. We experience less anxiety and more peace. We were created as spiritual beings, and when we fail to tap into the spiritual aspect of our lives, we often begin to feel a void in life. That void can produce feelings such as lacking joy or peace or being unsettled. To fill this void, I'd like to suggest that tapping into and engaging the spiritual asset of your life can bring a refreshing sense of hope and belonging. The spirituality asset account can be managed by setting aside time for reflection and meditation, reading affirming messages from spiritual authors, and fellowshipping with others who are also managing and adding to their spirituality asset account. These practices can help you find the center point of life, and no matter how crazy or challenging life can get, just like the calmest place is the eye or center of a storm or tornado, the most peaceful space in life is in the center of the will of your Creator and in fellowship with our spiritual being.

Inventory - Self Assessment.

In the accounting profession, because there are so many transactions that add to and subtract from inventory asset accounts, there is a greater risk that the value in the system for tracking the inventory asset does not match the value of the actual assets on hand. To verify the number of assets on hand and to ensure the system is updated, businesses schedule and execute regular inventory counts. During these counts, individuals manually count every item of inventory and ensure that the system is updated accordingly. In life, it is equally important that you take an inventory of your assets. While taking an inventory of your assets you should ask yourself, what are my life assets? And what is the value of my life assets? Because life assets are subjective, it may be easier to ask yourself if the value of your life assets are increasing or decreasing over time? This inventory assessment is also an opportunity for you to identify areas of your life that you may need to focus on more to increase the asset value. In finance, the most attractive companies to invest in are the ones that can display and maintain year over year growth. Even a stable company is one that may not necessarily be growing but is maintaining its current value. As the personal accountant of your life, you can decide whether you want to grow or just maintain; however, I believe we will get the most out of our lives as we strive to grow and increase our value. This would require daily decisions on how to increase the value in all of our asset accounts.

Chapter Five

Debt Free – Liabilities

L iability, not to be confused with reliability, is something that you will have to pay for either now or later. Whenever you receive an asset or something of value that you have not yet paid for, you have established a liability. A liability is something you owe or that will cost you in the future.

From a business or organization perspective, liabilities allow you to obtain assets without having the cash up front. Liabilities can be both short term and long term. In general, short term liabilities, are things that have to be paid within a year; whereas, long term liabilities can extend for much longer than one year. Most businesses have liabilities, and they hire qualified individuals to manage liabilities in relation to the equity and value of the business. Because there is no such thing as free money, most long term liabilities or debt are accompanied by interest expense, which is an additional charge for borrowing. In business, having liabilities alone is not a sign of instability. The key is proper management and the ability to pay back the liabilities at a future point in time. For example, a business with a large number of liabilities, very few assets, and lower equity is probably a business that one would question its ability to continue, pay the outstanding liabilities, and be profitable. On the contrary, a business that has reasonably managed liabilities or debt and continues to thrive with higher income and assets is probably seen as a sustainable business that will be able to pay back the debt.

In your personal finances, the amount of liabilities or debt that is considered to be good or reasonable is subjective. Mortgages for the purchase of a home or student loans for the expansion of your knowledge base are generally seen as "good debt." On the contrary, credit cards, pay day loans, and general financing opportunities, are sometimes seen as liabilities that are harder to pay back because they usually cost unreasonably more to borrow due to high interest rates. Scriptural guidance says that we should owe no man nothing but to love him (Romans 13:8 KJV). This can be hard when we live in a culture where we strive to keep up appearances and always want the next big thing, but we cannot afford to pay cash for it. It may be a challenge, but it is worth giving thought to how we can manage our finances in a way that we become totally debt free. I imagine that being debt free would also give us the ability to live worry-free and do all of the fun and exciting things we wish to do with our money.

In our personal lives, the liabilities, debt, and things that we owe to either ourselves or others can include forgiveness, apologies, empathy, respect, and love.

Forgiveness.

When we chose to harbor hurt feelings and bitter thoughts, we create a huge liability. Now, one accountant response may be, "Forgiveness is not a liability; it is an asset because someone OWES me an apology." Actually, we owe it to ourselves to forgive others. If we want to experience the fulfilled life that our Creator wants for us, we cannot harbor past hurts. If we want to move forward, we cannot look back to remember what everyone did against us.

Forgiveness is a liability because you owe it to both others and yourself to forgive. Why do you owe forgiveness to the person that hurt or wronged you? As empowered as we may feel and become over time, we are not the final judges of life, and we do not have divine authority to hold judgment over others who have made mistakes in life. In reality, the person who lives in divine perfection is the only one with the authority and ability to determine who does not have a chance at being forgiven, and to be honest, that perfect person forgives, too. This idea of forgiveness is colored by the golden rule. If we want others to forgive us, we should extend forgiveness to others. As hard as they may strive for perfection, some people make mistakes, knowingly and unknowingly. We have an obligation to highlight those mistakes so that they are made aware and are informed to make better decisions in the future. We can even proceed with caution in how we interact with them in the future as past experiences can inform future decisions. Nonetheless, we extend forgiveness to them so that they have the opportunity to pivot in life and begin to make better decisions going forward. When we choose not to forgive others, we hinder them from being able to reach the pivotal point of making better decisions in the future. Essentially, we put them in what I like to refer to as the deep ditch for the unforgiven where they cannot be redeemed and have no release to make better decisions. Their apologies cannot be heard from the ditch, and their new actions cannot be seen to prove any change of heart. When we send others to the unforgiveness ditch, we do them a genuine disservice, as we take away their opportunity for future change and reconciliation. Not only should we forgive others to free them from the ditch of unforgiveness, but we also have to forgive to free ourselves. See, when we put someone into the ditch, there is a cord that we hold to keeping them in the unforgiven ditch. This cord keeps us just as connected to the hurt and bound to the pain. We cannot fully move forward in our own lives because we refuse to let go of the cord that is holding someone else hostage. I have heard people say that you have to forgive for you, and this is true. The cord that you carry connected to the person in the ditch keeps you from sleeping peacefully and maneuvering through life comfortably. The person you are mad at has probably found a comfortable place to sleep in the ditch, but you may toss and turn because you cannot let go of a cord. I have intentionally depicted forgiveness as something as simple as letting go because we often try to make forgiveness such a difficult and insurmountable task. In reality, if we just let go of trying to keep someone else bound, we would free both them and ourselves in an instant so that we can go our separate ways and progress in our own individual lives. Refusing to forgive creates a huge liability and weight in our lives, but once we pay that debt we give ourselves the capacity to move forward and increase our accounting position. As a life accountant, the best way to manage this account, is to identify the people that you have placed in the ditch of unforgiveness. Then let go of the cord.

Apologies.

Along the lines of forgiveness, I cannot tell you how many times as a child I heard someone say, "you owe them an apology." I have listed apologies as a liability because if you have not apologized, it is something that you owe, but the key to apologizing is making sure you are apologizing for the right things to the right people.

Some people apologize for everything. "I'm sorry, I have plans and will not be able to attend your event." "I'm sorry, for walking into the room while you were speaking." "I apologize; I had a different perspective." In my opinion, these instances do not warrant an apology. If you have plans, you have no obligation to attend certain events. If you belong in the room and deserve a seat at the table, your presence is needed. If you have a different perspective, it should be shared. An apology is not necessarily warranted in these situations. As such, it is important to discern the appropriate times for apologies.

The key to apologizing is taking ownership. When you take full ownership, you pat yourself on the back when you experience success and apologize when you experience failures. Apologies are not meant to be pity parties, but instead are clear, concise communications of ownership that should be followed by a corrective action. Apologies should be short term liabilities only. If you owe someone an apology, you should do it now. The longer you wait to apologize the more time you leave for unforgiveness to fester. A timely apology is like having ointment and a band-aid on hand to apply right after an accident. Timeliness limits the chances for infection, but if you wait too long, bacteria could set into the injury causing it to take twice as long to heal. Also, apologizing to the wrong person is like putting the band-aid in the wrong place where there is no wound. Just as you would quickly apply a band-aid to the actual wound, apologies should be quick and to the person directly impacted by your mistake. While accounting for your life, it is important to manage the apology account by ensuring that as soon as you owe an apology, you identify to whom you owe it, and you give it, sincerely.

Empathy.

Now, you might be wondering why empathy is something that you owe, but in life, I have learned that if we lack empathy, we become selfish individuals who cannot receive all that life wants to offer us. Empathy is the innate ability to put yourself in the shoes of others, consider their "why," and show that you care. We all have different experiences and paths, but when we put ourselves in the shoes of others, we strive to understand where others are coming from before jumping to conclusions. This, in turn, challenges us to consider the reason for the behavior of others. In general, when someone does something that we do not like, we tend to quickly assume that their reason for doing it was derived from negative intentions. However, when we take an empathetic approach, we consider that maybe there was a perfectly reasonable explanation for the action. Think about when someone does not answer your phone call. Do you assume they missed your call because they are ignoring you or because they were in a difficult situation and could not get to the phone? In addition to assuming the worst with people that we fail to relate to, a lack of empathy often reveals itself in the failure to care about anyone other than ourselves. A self-centered universe positions itself at the core of its own demise. We cannot flourish in life if we do not relate to and help others around us. If we could excel in life in a silo, then we would not all be connected and intertwined through family trees, experiences, and purpose. Every created being has a purpose that is connected to another created being, and when we fail to exercise empathy, we jeopardize our ability to experience the fullness of life. The ability to display empathy is in our nature, but the practice of being empathic must be the result of an intentional decision. As accountants, we have to train ourselves to choose empathetic responses in every situation. If we do not practice this, our empathy liability account will continue to grow over time, and we will find that our purpose connections are strained in such a way that we cannot receive all that life has to offer us.

Respect.

Like forgiveness, respect is a liability that you owe both to yourself and others. People who respect themselves protect themselves. Since I have already made the case that your life has value, I will not belabor the point, but in general, when you recognize your value, you respect yourself. A level of self-respect is triggered when self-worth is known. Respecting oneself includes being mindful of how you speak to yourself, where you allow yourself to go, and what you allow yourself to do. A measure of self-control, self-preservation, and protection is the result of self-respect.

Respecting others is just as important as respecting oneself. I am of the belief that respect does not have to necessarily be earned. The fact that an individual is a human with a valuable life and a divine purpose is reason enough to respect them. Someone does not have to be an authority figure or have a certain status to earn respect. From the janitor to the president, from the child to the disrespectful boss – everyone deserves respect. In my life, I have learned the importance of not repaying disrespect with disrespect. There are some disrespectful and rude people in the world, but their actions do not reduce your liability to respond respectfully. Because you are the accountant of your life, your responses and reactions are what impact your liabilities. It is not fair to yourself or the financial position of your life to have it decreased because someone disrespected you. You have the power to choose your response to upsetting events in a way that does not negatively impact your life accounting. Choose to be respectful in all situations. If anything, this choice may strike your offender as intriguing, and they may strive to be more respectful in the future.

Love.

As mentioned earlier, the perspective of our Creator is that the only liability that we should owe is to love (Romans 13:8 KJV). I believe that this love should be for ourselves and others. The ability to fully love oneself is directly related to recognizing the value of oneself. Once you understand and accept your true value, you can love yourself deeply. Only after you truly love yourself, can you love your neighbor unconditionally. Furthermore, loving your neighbor helps them to recognize their value and to continue the sharing of love. Close your eyes and imagine a world where everyone knew and understood how to both give and receive love. I imagine there being such unity, harmony, and genuine support. Now, open your eyes and look in the mirror. Creating a world of love starts with you. Every day, as you account for your life, you have a liability of loving yourself and others, and throughout each day you should pay it off by loving effortlessly and unconditionally.

So, as you continue to account for your life, ask yourself these questions: Do you possess any other liabilities? What are some things that you owe to yourself or others? What are the practical steps that you can take to reduce your liabilities?

CHAPTER SIX

Revenue Generator

A revenue generator is essentially the source of your revenue. What are you doing to obtain more wealth? Financially and personally?

Financially, a source of income or revenue can be the service you provide on your job or personal investments. Business revenue generators can be goods, services, or investments. For most people and in business, the goal is to maximize revenue. The more revenue you generate, the better. In business, revenue is generally calculated by multiplying the number of goods sold or hours worked by the unit price or rate. The questions to ask in these instances for how to increase revenue would be: How do you increase revenue? How do you sell more products? The answer is two-fold: either increase the number of hours worked or goods sold or increase the price or rate.

Because revenue is calculated based on factors of multiplication, the best way to increase revenue is to increase one of the respective factors. Some of the benefits to having higher revenues include having more money to increase financial position, to spend or invest, to generate even more income, or to give to shareholders.

When accounting for your life personally, revenue represents victories in life. If you desire to have more victories and revenue, then you must first determine the factors for those victories and how you can increase them. Victories in life can be every day wins, overcoming difficult challenges, or reaching long term goals. Your achievements may be different than your neighbors and friends, but that does not mean they are not victories.

So, how can you increase the number of victories you have in life? First, change your perspective. There may be some things in your life that you may consider to be failures, and they are actually victories. Every trial, tribulation, and closed door that you may experience are not necessarily failures; they could be victories depending on your perspective.

I will share specific examples from my life that some may say are failures, but I am self-convinced that they are victories. First, the rejection letter that I received from the first university graduate program that I applied to could have been considered a failure; however, that rejection letter forced me to apply to another university, which I later attended. While attending, the second university of my choosing because of a seemingly failed attempt at life, I was able to obtain local field work experience while getting my second degree and living rent-free at home, which would not have been possible had I attended my first choice. In addition, I met my now husband at the new university. Yes, my life would have probably followed an entirely different path had I not experienced that initial rejection, but was the rejection a failure? I believe it was quite the opposite; it was one of the most defining, pivotal and victorious moments in my life. The second example that comes to mind is when I was laid off from my job; this too was probably one of my greatest life victories. That lay off alone afforded me the time and the resources to adequately study for and pass the Certified Public Accountant exam in a 3-month period. After which, I obtained employment with one of the Big Four public accounting firms. In both instances, I could have stopped at the rejection or layoff and deemed myself a failure. I could have quit at life because of those disappointments, but the beauty of life accounting is that I just had to keep living and the victory began to unfold itself right before my eyes. If you need help seeing your failures as victories, whenever you think you are failing, ask yourself, "What can I gain from this experience?" It may not always be a spouse, a certification, or a distinguished job, but I am confident that you will gain something specifically good for you. Depending on perspective, a shut door could be protection from a wrong door, an eye-opener to other open doors, or a warning sign of a dead end. A "no," does not have to necessarily be a "no." It could be a "not yet" or a "no, this is better." When you shift your perspective, what you used to consider to be failures in your life can be seen as victorious revenue generators. Sometimes, it only takes a paradigm shift to increase your net worth.

When it's not simply a perspective shift needed, other ways to increase the number of victories in your life are in the revenue factors such as positive attitudes, good deeds, giving your best, and endurance.

Positive attitude.

Have you ever heard the saying, "Your attitude determines your altitude"? It is true. Your attitude, demeanor, tone, and outlook are a reflection of where you will go in life. Attitude is a by-product of choice. You can choose whether or not to maintain a positive attitude. Because your attitude projects your altitude, having a positive attitude propels you to victorious living. Positivity is the ultimate revenue generator because no matter what happens to deplete you, if you maintain a positive outlook, it cannot negatively affect you. The challenge with having a positive attitude is that sometimes positivity can isolate you in a culture where people thrive from complaining and harboring ill will. You may not want to be considered "Negative Nelly," but at the same time, you don't want to be so positively optimistic that you escape reality. Having a positive attitude does not mean that you ignore life challenges or difficult people. It means that you choose to respond to those challenges with positivity.

Not only is a positive attitude a revenue generator that brings you victory in even the most tumultuous times, but a positive attitude can reduce stress and could positively impact your health. As the accountant of your life, it is important to be intentional about your attitude choice. Choose to maintain a positive attitude and notice the number of victories in life will accumulate over time.

Good deeds.

Performing a good deed is another effective way to increase revenue. When you are doing something positive and impactful for someone else, you are multiplying revenue in both your life and in the lives of the people that you help. Doing good for others is rewarding in and of itself. Seeing someone smile because of something that you have done is infectious. Good deeds could involve sharing your resources, investing time, or even giving advice or perspective. The key to effectively executing a good deed is first recognizing that you have something that someone else could benefit from. Once you identify what it is that you have to give, then you should find someone to share it with. The other special quality of good deeds is that there are no strings attached. You can multiply revenue just by doing good deeds alone; you don't have to expect something in return because the doing is what has given you the win in life. You win, when others benefit. I know this may be contrary to orthodox thinking, but sharing with others does not result in a loss. Giving does not produce lack. In actuality, these good deeds can multiply what you originally had to give and even give you more joy and fulfillment than you previously had. This is possible because the most fulfilled life is the life poured out doing good for others.

Giving your best.

In sports and life, the most victorious winners are the ones who always give their best. We get out of life what we put into it. So, if we invest mediocre inputs into our lives, then we should expect a mediocre outcome. However, when we give our best, we can expect the best that life has to offer. As the accountant of your life seeking to increase revenues, you should ensure that every area of your life is getting the best you. If you cannot give your best to everything that you put your hands to, then you should re-evaluate whether you should be doing it. This can be difficult, as you may have to make some challenging adjustments, but the victory you have to gain out of life cannot be maximized when you are stretched too thin. Evaluate your life, and ask yourself if you are giving your best. If the answer is yes, then keep generating revenue in your life, but if the answer is no, identify the adjustments that you need to make to increase the revenues of your life.

Endurance.

The final revenue generator that I will discuss is endurance. The ability to endure can be the difference between a victory and a failure in life. Every life has challenges, but victory and the ability to overcome is on the other side of endurance. You will never win if you give up. To make matters more complex, we are often closer to victory in life when challenges are the hardest. Let's look at this from the perspective of a race. In the beginning, everyone is off to a great start and running at full speed. However, towards the finish line, some have quit, and others may feel like the end is unreachable. Nonetheless, the one who presses through to the end with stomach and leg cramps and out of breath is the one who wins. Never let discomfort keep you from crossing the finish line because there is nothing sweeter than the taste of victory. Also, if you do not endure to the end and finish, you would have wasted a lot of time and assets and have no revenue to show for it. As the accountant of your life, only you can finish for you, so you have to make intentional strides towards your goals and purpose no matter the obstacles or challenges that you may be facing. Your life's revenue depends on your persistence and endurance. The only real way that you can fail at life is if you stop trying to win.

So, think about your life. How are you actively increasing your revenues? Are there other factors and revenue generators that you should be tapping into?

CHAPTER SEVEN

Expenses

E xpenses can easily reduce all the good that we do and the revenue that we generate in life. Expenses in business are the costs of doing business. Whether it is what you pay to keep the lights on or employees satisfied, the additional interest that you pay to borrow, or the costs to make a product, expenses are deducted from revenue to determine your net financial position. If expenses are greater than revenues, the company is said to be operating at a loss, but because the general goal of a business is to be profitable, companies have to manage expenses to ensure that they are proportionately lower than the revenue earned.

In life, expenses are the things that reduce the value of our lives and take away from our revenues earned. If we do not account for our lives appropriately, we can devalue ourselves by investing more time creating expenses than we do generating revenue. Expenses consist of the negative things that we do, negative things that we say, failure to move toward purpose or the failure to accept grace.

Negative things done.

Expenses can be the negative things that we do to ourselves and others. This includes any act of hate, ill-will, or pride. They say actions speak louder than words, so even if you only speak pleasantries, if your actions are full of negativity, your expense account will continue to grow. The adverse actions that we do cannot only negatively impact our life accounting, but they can also create negative reactions. This means that just as positivity can multiply, negativity can multiply in your life, as well. As the accountant of your life, it is imperative to be aware of how your actions will impact the equity of your life. Thinking before executing an action is the best way to manage and minimize expenses. If we always react and go with our initial heated response, we may find ourselves accumulating more expenses that we would like, but the pause before an action could be the difference between a positive or negative net financial position in life.

Negative things said.

Another easy way to increase the expense account and devalue your life is to speak negatively about yourself. Although actions speak louder than words, words have the power to change your life. If you consistently say what you cannot and will not do or if you speak failure, lack, and death over your life, you will surely experience all of the above. In addition, if you allow comparison to be the barometer of your life, you may find yourself saying or thinking that you are of less value than your neighbors and friends. Just as words have power, before they become words, even as you think in your heart, so you will be (Proverbs 23:7 KJV). This is probably much easier said than done, but to decrease the number of expenses in your life, you should also arrest all negative thoughts and choose to think positively about yourself and others. No matter where you want to go in life, you cannot get there if your mind is not focused. This is because action starts in our hearts, travels to our mind, comes out of our mouths, and then moves our bodies. Even if an action skips our mouths, it still gets its direction from our minds. So, what are you thinking right now? Were the last words that came out of your mouth revenue generating or an expense? The interesting thing about life and our tongues is that there is no neutral zone.

Either we are appropriately accounting for our lives and increasing on all angles, or we are allowing liabilities and expenses to overshadow us. When we speak, either it is positive and revenue generating, or it is negative and expensive. As an informed life accountant, you should determine the accounting impact of your words before you speak them.

Failure to move towards purpose.

Let us be reminded, that we were all created with a unique purpose, so if we go through life and fail to complete our objective of living, that is the ultimate expense. Going through life not identifying or striving to complete our purpose is essentially wasting our existence and snubbing our Creator. One way to expense a life is to not use it. When we sit down instead of serving or shut up instead of encouraging, we are expensing our lives. We were created for a purpose and given a value from our Create to execute. When we go through life failing to fulfill our purpose or not recognizing and sharing our value, it will greatly expense our life, and we will eventually die full, yet empty. So how do you identify your purpose? The first way is to ask your Creator. Secondly, ask yourself what you are passionate about. Your passions are directly related to what you were created to do. Lastly, begin to imagine yourself helping someone. What are you doing? This is probably a step towards fulfilling your purpose.

As the accountant of your life, it is your responsibility to identify your purpose, so that you can begin to live and thrive. Until you connect with your purpose, you merely exist in a world, but once you begin to live in purpose, you will find accounting for your life to be much easier. Accounting will be easier because it will be connected to more than just another to do list. It will be connected to helping you to reach the point of being the best you so that you can become an asset to someone else.

Failure to identify and strive for purpose can lead to depression and the feeling of emptiness and worthlessness, but that does not have to be your destiny. Every day that you wake is another opportunity to reverse this expense and begin to live a purpose-driven and victorious life.

Failure to accept grace.

This is the final expense that I will explore because the beauty of life is that as long as you are living this life, you have the opportunity to accept grace and begin again. Grace is the gift to start today no matter what you may have done yesterday. While reading this book, you may have recognized that you have more liabilities than assets, and you may feel as though you are drowning in a sea of expenses. No matter how ineffective you have been at accounting for your life in past, you have the gift of grace to begin again today. The only way you can fail at accounting for your life is if you fail to accept the opportunity of grace to begin again. Failing to accept grace is simply accepting self-defeat, but there is no level of defeat that grace cannot reach. As the accountant of your life, you are in control of the actions, thoughts, and habits that impact the value of your life, and if you struggled last week, you can begin again this week. This concept of grace gives you permission to forgive yourself, make new commitments and decisions, and turn your life around at any moment. As long as you accept this gift, you give yourself resilience in your day to day life accounting.

As you can see, expenses decrease your value, but they do not have to be a dead end for your life. As the accountant of your life, you still have the opportunity to choose to reduce expenses, and increase revenues, so that you can begin to get the most out of life.

CHAPTER EIGHT

Budget vs. Actual

In the accounting world, most businesses create a financial budget for the year and concurrently track progress against that budget as the year progresses. Budgeting positions the business to make financially disciplined spending decisions so that it can reach a desired financial position. To develop a budget, accountants partner with the business to obtain the assumptions and plan for the year. This plan can include how much is expected to be earned in revenues as well as the expected costs to be incurred. The budget is then reviewed and adjusted to ensure a reasonable net financial position. Budgets can be developed at a daily, weekly, monthly, quarterly, or annual level. In my experience, a monthly budget is the most effective because it allows for reasonably frequent check-ins to measure progress and make decisions to ensure that the annual budgeting goals are met. Budgets are managed in business by developing reports to compare and analyze actual revenues and spending to the planned or budgeted amounts. During this analyzing phase, if variances are identified, accountants should partner with the business to determine why the actuals are not in line with the budget. The reasons for actual variances could be due to timing, a change in business plan, or the impact of external factors that were not included in the original budget assumptions. Nonetheless, identifying these variances monthly, gives the business time to make any necessary adjustments, so that the net position for the year is positive.

I discussed the importance for budgeting personal finances in the chapter on assets, so I will not belabor the point other than encouraging you to position yourself to tell your money where to go versus ending every year wondering where all of your money went. Budgeting puts you into a position of control.

Likewise, creating a personal budget for your life allows you to set goals for progressing in life and increasing the equity of your life. Once you have completed and evaluated your budget for reasonableness, you can begin to make financial and personal life decisions that are in line with your budget. In addition, when you take the time to compare your actual life to your budgeted life, you may highlight the areas of your life where you may need to exercise more self-control. Whether it is excessively spending, being rude, giving up, or speaking negatively, variances to the budget will reveal opportunities to exercise more discipline. When you make the appropriate decisions to ensure you meet or exceed your expectations from life, you are truly benefiting from budgeting. Budgeting is only effective if you intentionally follow through with your actions to meet the budget.

Create your life budget.

Imagine what your best self looks like. What is the ideal value of your assets, liabilities, revenues, and expenses? Starting with waking up in the morning, moving on to your interactions throughout the day, and concluding with your accomplishments by the time you lay down for the night, what has your best self done? Record the activities and achievements of your best self, and this will become your budget for life. Notice, that I did not suggest you choose someone that you want to be like and make their life the budget for your life. This is because comparison can become a slippery slope and slowly steal your satisfaction with yourself. You were not created to be anyone other than you, so when creating the budget for your life, it is imperative that you start envisioning *your* best self. The best version of you is everything that makes you who you are multiplied by positivity and divided into sharing you with the world. The goal of budgeting is not to highlight everything you are not. Instead, you are setting goals for who you will become with focused energy and intentional decisions.

Budget vs. Actual.

Once you have developed the budget of your life, take an introspective look at your actual life vs. your best-self life. The differences are just opportunities for enhancement that will position you to get the most out of life. For every difference that you identify, I suggest developing a realistic goal, a word of encouragement, and someone to hold you accountable. Goals can be tricky if they are too far-fetched, but a realistic goal is something that you know you can do with the right amount of effort. Once you set the goal, partner the goal with words that you can use to encourage yourself along the journey of completing the goal. These words will help you to continue to push on the days that you feel like giving up. These words will also remind you that you can become your best self. Lastly, we have already discussed the importance of accountability partners, but having someone who will check in with you and encourage you along the way is priceless.

Results.

Becoming your best self is a moment by moment process. It will not be achieved over night, but be patient with yourself in the process. As you reach goals of betterment, you will reassess your life and redefine your best self, which will result in new goals. As you stay committed to trying, encouraging yourself, and asking for help, you will notice progress in your life over time. The beauty of living and achieving budgeted results is the renewed sense of being that follows. In life, once you achieve a goal, you do not stop; you create a new goal. Continuing to press toward success makes you even better than the initial best self that you envisioned for yourself. The most successful companies are those who increase income year over year. That is what we should strive for in life – continuous and progressive results. As life accountants, start where you are with today's budget, but do not be surprised when you look back years from now and see that you have far exceeded all budgeted expectations and are continuing to create assets, increase revenue, and sustain positive equity.

CHAPTER NINE

Internal Controls

A n internal control is a process or procedure that is designed to prevent or detect mistakes or fraud. In the accounting world, internal controls became a requirement as a result of uncovered financial misrepresentation that was not reported or identified by the public accounting profession. The Sarbanes Oxley Act of 2002 was created by the United States Congress to protect investors from fraudulent accounting activities by corporations. Sections 302 and 404 of the Act require management to ensure adequate and effective internal controls are in place to reasonably detect or prevent accounting misstatements. There are two types of internal controls: detective and preventive. Detective controls are designed to detect mistakes or fraud. These are generally review controls where someone reviews and approves transactions. On the other hand, preventive controls are controls designed to prevent actions that could result in misstatements. An example of preventative control would be limiting access to accounting systems for unscreened individuals. The other important aspect of these controls is that they are the internal responsibility of the business's management. Management does not have the luxury of saying that external auditors are responsible for ensuring their internal controls are adequate. Management must represent to the governing bodies, that they have internally tested and verified that they have adequate controls that are operating effectively.

We are the managers and accountants of our personal lives, and thus we are responsible for ensuring that we have and adhere to internal controls and boundaries to keep us on track in our lives. I have identified six internal controls of life that I believe will protect us from becoming victims of fraudulent activities that seek to misrepresent our progress in accounting for our lives. The controls are 1) listening to your gut, 2) being honest, 3) saying No, 4) thinking first 5) requesting feedback, and 6) removing the option to quit.

Listening to your gut.

We have been gifted a still, small voice that nudges us, directs us, and guides us. Some call it the spirit of our Creator, others refer to it as a feeling, but today I will call it the gut. It is a deep down knowing in the center of your belly, and if we listen and adhere to it, it will guide us into all truth (John 16:13 KJV). The amazing thing about the gut is that it is always aware and trying to direct us in life, but we often drown it out with our thoughts and opinions. As we maneuver through life as accountants, there will be temptations and opportunities to choose to act in ways that will deplete our assets and increase our expenses. Because we were not created to live in silos, our lives can be impacted by the mistakes of others, and we can find ourselves aimlessly being tossed to and from with our emotions. In these moments, it is easy to forget you are the accountant of your life, and increasing liabilities could become the inherent impact of your decisions. With no accountability partner close by and a disparity of hope, the self-preserving internal control that you can rely on to keep you grounded is the still, small voice of your gut. Your gut may tell you to rest, or it may tell you to get up and move, but your gut can be trusted because it is informed by the motives of your Creator. Your gut is inside of your being, but it has the DNA of your Creator. It knows the best decision that you should make, and the places in life that you should steer away from. The goal of your gut is to protect you from value depleting choices and to guide you into a purpose driven and fulfilling life. So, if you ever feel you have lost control of life or are confused about what decisions to make, listen to your gut. It is an internal control that will not lead you astray.

Being honest.

You cannot effectively keep track of life and progress if there is no honesty about where you are. If you have convinced your broken self that you have all the assets and revenues that life has to offer, then you are less likely to strive for more, and you will remain depleted. Being honest with yourself and others is equally important. Tell yourself what you need to hear to be motivated, and tell others what they need to hear to become better. There is no good way to lie because withholding the truth is imprisoning. When you fail to be honest, you do not give yourself or others the freedom to pivot and make better decisions going forward. This internal control of honesty will open the door for you to define opportunity and be free to become a better you.

Saying no.

As we navigate through life, there will be countless opportunities to go here or there or to do this or that. I can almost guarantee you that there will be more opportunities than you have time for. The internal control that will save you from attending without purpose is saying no. One of the principles that I use to determine what to say no to in life is connecting the dots. If what I am being asked to do does not have a connection to the purpose of my life and is not asset producing or revenue generating, then I have clear justification for saying no. So, the next time something comes up, look for the dots connecting you to purpose and a positive equity balance. If the dots are not there, you are probably safe saying no. It is worth noting that every positive thing in the world is not necessarily connected to your specific purpose or contributing to the equity balance of your life. Carefully evaluate opportunities because you do not want to expend your life doing good things that do not positively impact the financials of your life.

Thinking first.

This is the internal control that will keep you from flying off the edges when people disrespect you. Before you react, think. Think about what you are about to say or do, and reflect on the net impact of what you plan to say or do. Once you have thought through your reaction and noted the potential consequences, then choose the less harmful reaction. I have had instances in my life where I reacted first and thought about it later, and each time I wish I had acted differently. There are some really mean people in the world who do unjust things, but their actions do not give us a license to be mean. We are still the accountants of our lives, and we need to account for both our actions and reactions appropriately. In the most heated moments, training yourself to take a minute to think before you react can save you in the future. Be reminded that in that moment, you are not simply thinking of how you will react, but you are also thinking about the net impact of that decision. For example, if your boss has lied about you, your immediate reaction may be to call him a liar and tell him off. In the minute of thinking, you may consider that telling your boss off is grounds for termination, so you may decide to share with your boss the truth in a very calm and respectful tone, or maybe even say nothing at all. The point is that taking the minute to think may have both saved your job and other's opinions and perceptions of you. Imagine how the news of you cursing out your boss would spread throughout your company – like wildfire. Sometimes the justifiable immediate reaction is not worth the reputational damage, so think first.

Requesting feedback.

Internal controls are meant to keep you on track as you account for your life. Sometimes we have an obscured view of our progress, so it is helpful to request feedback from a third party. This third party can be clients, peers, mentors, family, or friends. The feedback will help you to identify your blind spots or help you to recognize that you are doing better than you may have thought. It can be daunting to ask for feedback for fear that it will always be negative, but the most beneficial feedback has balance. It highlights both what you do well and where you can improve. Requesting and obtaining this feedback will help you to know what to continue and what to tweak, and the result is a better you. You cannot get the most out of life if you are stagnant; however, requesting feedback is a way for you to move beyond your comfort zone and into a new dimension of your fulfilling life.

One of my most memorable feedback experiences taught me that I determine whether I face obstacles or opportunities in life. Sometimes in life we experience challenges and face difficult people, but how we choose to see these things will determine whether they are obstacles or opportunities. Obstacles block progress, but opportunities provide options for movement. When I encountered a person of ill intentions, I sought out feedback. I asked for input on my past responses and advice for future encounters. The most repetitive theme of the feedback that I received was that although I could not control the individual, I could control how much power I gave them over my life. I could decide that they would not be an obstacle to keep me from achieving my long-term goals. I could also decide that they would be an opportunity for me to master dealing with difficult people and to note how not to treat others in the future. Based on the feedback I received, I gained a key asset of wisdom from that negative experience even if the intention of the aggressor was to deplete me. Feedback is your friend while accounting for your life. It gives you new perspectives and points you towards opportunities.

Removing the option to quit.

The last internal control that I will describe is removing the option to quit. When quitting is not an option, you have no choice but to continue living, striving, and accounting for your life. Throughout this book, I have not shied away from the fact that life is not always easy. Whether we need a mindset shift or a perspective change, we can overcome if we try. The moment we stop trying is the moment we quit on ourselves, our Creator, and the people who are counting on us to succeed. Because our lives are connected, if I quit, then the person who needs me experiences a void, and if they in turn quit, then the children who need them are lacking. There is a trickle-down effect to quitting, and that is why the imperative internal control to ensure you live your best life is removing the option to quit. Do not give yourself the option, and do not entertain the thought. You cannot quit because your life has a value that cannot be replaced in the world. The world needs you to strap up your boots and go to work. Work on being the best version of you.

As we aim to account for our lives, we should make a conscious effort to surround our lives with effective internal controls to keep us on track for fulfilling our purpose. Distractions are set up for us on a daily basis, but these internal controls protect our minds and hearts. After we have successfully identified and fortified the internal controls in our lives, every day is an opportunity to see the adequacy and effectiveness of those controls.

In addition to living a well-controlled life that protects our value, we should also strive to be an internal control in the lives of others. Nothing that we have learned or experienced in our lives is solely for us. Others can learn from our experiences, and we can give feedback and encouragement to help them continue on the course of accounting for their lives, as well. After all, the value of life is the gift that continues to give. When you effectively account for your life, you have something of value to share, that in turn adds to the value of the next person's life. Internal controls safeguard your value so that the cycle can continue.

CHAPTER TEN

Financial Statement Presentation

Financial statements are a summary detail of the financial position of an entity. Companies can create and distribute financial statements monthly, quarterly or annually. The purpose of financial statements is to give the reader a summarized perspective of the entities financial position. These statements show the value of your assets, the amount of debt incurred, revenues, and expenses. Banks review these statements to determine whether to loan the entity money, and stockholders review these statements to evaluate whether the company is a good investment. These statements are designed to tell the true story of an entity's financial position.

In life, your financial statements are presented every day when you interact with others. How you treat them, what you say, how you think, and how you behave are all a display of your personal financial position. Contrary to what some may think, your financial position is not only displayed in those obvious "do right moments" of attending a local church, volunteering at a food bank, or giving a charitable donation. The true essence of your financial position is displayed when the circumstances of your situation are not so black and white. Whether you are dealing with a negative coworker, stuck behind a slow driver on the highway, passing a beggar at a stop light, or hanging out with friends, what you do and say in these moments is the true unedited version of your financial position.

When people see you, what do they see? How is the atmosphere of a room changed when you enter? When someone hears you speak, do they notice a positive or negative difference? Do your actions match what you say? Are you someone that people desire to be around? Based on your presentation of yourself, do you appear to be rich in love, kindness, and positivity? Or do you seem to have emotional liabilities?

The interesting thing about your financial presentation is that it is what it is. Sometimes you can try to appear to be a pleasant and positive person, but when the fire is blazing, the rubber meets the road, or someone upsets you, your reaction will unveil your true position. The only way to truly change your financial presentation is to go back to the individual line items and accounts that make up the statements. In business, a company cannot legally change the numbers to portray income that has not been earned. The auditors will write them up and give them a bad opinion. The same is true in life. Never try to short change the process by presenting yourself as something you are not. Be honest with yourself and listen to what your thoughts and actions in difficult situations tell you about yourself. There is always something that you can try to work on to steadily increase your wealth.

Generally, companies hire external auditors to come and audit their financial statements so that they can make any necessary adjustments to ensure they correctly represent their financial position. Our goal in accounting for our lives is to audit our financials to highlight the areas where we are lacking and can make adjustments to ensure that we exhibit wealth at all times. Accountability partners, mentors, and spiritual leaders can be great life auditors; however, we should also audit ourselves and be transparent with ourselves because that is the first step to acknowledging the need for change and making progress toward a better financial position.

I have had situations in life that showed me my financial position. In the moment, it felt like I was looking in a mirror and seeing one too many flaws, but the good thing about these flaws was that I had the power within to change them. Financial presentation unveils the deep things of your heart. Maybe I was not as kind and patient as I thought I was. The good news is that life did not end there. As the accountant of my life, I could make new choices to add assets and revenues and decrease liabilities and expenses in the future.

Financial Statement Presentation – Legacy.

The ultimate review of our financial statement presentation will be in our death. What legacy will we leave? How many people will be impacted? Will we leave assets for our children or will they be left in debt? I mean this both literally and figuratively.

Will we have lived a financially responsible life and left our children an estate that can be passed down for generations? Or will we just leave them with unpaid bills and funeral costs? Consider the impact of these two scenarios: one outcome may be grateful descendants with peace of mind and the other, stressed descendants with little hope for tomorrow. What legacy will you leave?

Have you stayed on a budget to increase revenues and assets and reduce expenses and liabilities? Will your descendants speak of the legacy of love and the positive financial statement that you left them? Or will your memory be one of discontent and self-centeredness? In our death, we should want people to benefit from our value and pursue a life of positive accounting.

If you are reading this book, it is not too late for you to begin accounting for your life. Today you can begin making positive accounting decisions to increase the equity of your life. You have a purpose and others are depending on your legacy.

Certified Life
Accounant™

Upon completion of reading and applying the text of *Accounting for Your Life*, you gain an irrevocable certification. You are a CERTIFIED LIFE ACCOUNTANT™ (CLA). In the business world, individuals have to pass examinations and pay fees to become Certified Public Accountants, and the certification gives them the authority to provide exclusive services and give opinions on the financial statements of companies. Enduring life's experiences and choosing to overcome are what qualifies you to become a CERTIFIED LIFE ACCOUNTANT™. Your choice to intentionally account for your life has granted you the authority to control the financial position of your life.

Certification Pledge

As the CLA of your life, I ask that you complete and sign this pledge: I _____, do solemnly promise to execute my role as a CERTIFIED LIFE ACCOUNTANT™ to the best of my ability. I will evaluate the balances in my life accounts. I will strive to increase the equity of my life while fulfilling my purpose. I will contribute positively to the lives of others. I will not quit.

_____

(Signature)

APPENDIX

CERTIFIED LIFE ACCOUNTANT™ FORM

REVIEW OF ASSETS

In the space provided below list your life assets.

_____

_____

_____

_____

_____

_____

_____

_____

In the space provided below document ways that you can debit (increase) the assets listed above.

_____

_____

_____

_____

_____

_____

_____

_____

_____

In the space provided below document the things that may credit (decrease) the assets listed above.

_____

_____

_____

_____

_____

_____

_____

_____

_____

_____

_____

In the space provided below identify additional assets that you would like to add to your life.

_____

_____

_____

_____

_____

_____

_____

_____

_____

_____

_____

CERTIFIED LIFE ACCOUNTANT™ FORM

REVIEW OF ASSETS

In the space provided below list your life assets.

_____

_____

_____

_____

_____

_____

_____

_____

_____

In the space provided below document ways that you can debit (increase) the assets listed above.

_____

_____

_____

_____

_____

_____

_____

_____

_____

_____

In the space provided below document the things that may credit (decrease) the assets listed above.

_____
_____
_____
_____
_____
_____
_____
_____
_____
_____
_____

In the space provided below identify additional assets that you would like to add to your life.

_____
_____
_____
_____
_____
_____
_____
_____
_____
_____
_____

CERTIFIED LIFE ACCOUNTANT™ FORM

REVIEW OF LIABILITIES

In the space provided below list your life liabilities.

_____

_____

_____

_____

_____

_____

_____

_____

_____

_____

In the space provided below document ways that you can debit (decrease) the liabilities listed above.

_____

_____

_____

_____

_____

_____

_____

_____

_____

_____

_____

In the space provided below document the things that may credit (increase) the liabilities listed above.

CERTIFIED LIFE ACCOUNTANT™ FORM

REVIEW OF LIABILITIES

In the space provided below list your life liabilities.

In the space provided below document ways that you can debit (decrease) the liabilities listed above.

In the space provided below document the things that may credit (increase) the liabilities listed above.

_____

_____

_____

_____

_____

_____

_____

_____

_____

_____

_____

_____

_____

CERTIFIED LIFE ACCOUNTANT™ FORM

REVIEW OF REVENUE

In the space provided below list your revenue factors.

_____
_____
_____
_____
_____
_____
_____
_____
_____
_____
_____

In the space provided below document ways that you can credit (increase) the revenue of your life.

_____
_____
_____
_____
_____
_____
_____
_____
_____
_____
_____
_____

CERTIFIED LIFE ACCOUNTANT™ FORM

REVIEW OF REVENUE

In the space provided below list your revenue factors.

In the space provided below document ways that you can credit (increase) the revenue of your life.

CERTIFIED LIFE ACCOUNTANT™ FORM

REVIEW OF EXPENSES

In the space provided below list your current expenses.

_____

_____

_____

_____

_____

_____

_____

_____

_____

_____

_____

In the space provided below document ways that you can credit (decrease) the expenses of your life.

_____

_____

_____

_____

_____

_____

_____

_____

_____

_____

_____

CERTIFIED LIFE ACCOUNTANT™ FORM

REVIEW OF EXPENSES

In the space provided below list your current expenses.

_____

_____

_____

_____

_____

_____

_____

_____

_____

_____

_____

In the space provided below document ways that you can credit (decrease) the expenses of your life.

_____

_____

_____

_____

_____

_____

_____

_____

_____

_____

_____

CERTIFIED LIFE ACCOUNTANT™ FORM

BUDGET vs. ACTUAL

In the space provided below list the attributes of your budget (best-self) as well as how you actually measure against those items. Where you have opportunity, develop a realistic goal to help you achieve your budget.

BUDGET (Best-self)	ACTUAL	GOAL

CERTIFIED LIFE ACCOUNTANT™ FORM

BUDGET vs. ACTUAL

In the space provided below list the attributes of your budget (best-self) as well as how you actually measure against those items. Where you have opportunity, develop a realistic goal to help you achieve your budget.

BUDGET (Best-self)	ACTUAL	GOAL

CERTIFIED LIFE ACCOUNTANT™ FORM

FINANCIAL STATEMENT PRESENTATION

In the space provided below define your purpose and the legacy you aspire to leave.

_____

_____

_____

_____

_____

_____

_____

_____

_____

_____

_____

_____

_____

_____

_____

_____

_____

_____

CERTIFIED LIFE ACCOUNTANT™ FORM

FINANCIAL STATEMENT PRESENTATION

In the space provided below define your purpose and the legacy you aspire to leave.